Copyright © 2021 by Ingo Blum
www.ingoblumbooks.com
All rights reserved. No part of this publication may be reproduced, distributed or transmitted in any form or by any means, including photocopying, recording, or other electronic or mechanical methods, without the prior written permission of the publisher, except in the case of brief quotations embodied in critical reviews and certain other noncommercial uses permitted by copyright law. For permission requests, write to the publisher, addressed "Attention: Permissions Coordinator," at the address below. Thanks!

published by planetOh concepts,
www.planetohconcepts.com

Publisher`s Note:
Please note that the French and English versions of the story were written to be as close as possible. However, in some cases they may differ in order to accomodate the nuances and fluidity of each language. Author, translator, and publisher made every effort to ensure accuracy. We therefore take no responsibility for inconsistency and minor errors.

Illustrated by Mark Nino Balita
Book layout by Emy Farella
Translated by Kind Words Translations
Proofread by Lea Kaul

First Edition 2021 - ISBN: 978-3-947410-15-6

Ingo Blum

DON'T BE SCARED!
N'aie pas peur!

Illustrated by
Mark Nino Balita

Today, Susie's mother wants to bake a cake for the family.

She sends Susie to the village to get some butter, flour, and cherries for the cake.

But Susie is scared.

Aujourd'hui, la mère de Susie veut faire un gâteau pour la famille.

Elle envoie Susie au village pour acheter du beurre, de la farine et des cerises pour le gâteau.

Mais Susie a peur.

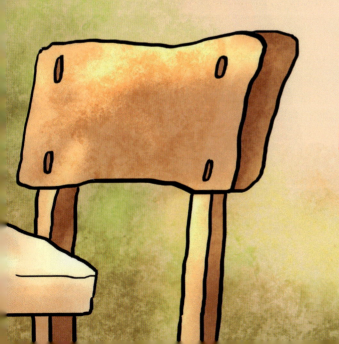

She is scared of the angry ghost behind her parents' house.

Elle a peur du méchant fantôme derrière la maison de ses parents.

When she crosses a big field of barley, she hears a whisper. The whisper comes from the scarecrows in the field, who seem to be watching Susie.

Quand elle traverse un grand champ d'orge, elle entend un murmure. Le murmure vient des épouvantails dans le champ qui semblent être en train de regarder Susie.

She is scared of the forest because it is dark and full of mysterious shadows.

Elle a peur de la forêt. La forêt est sombre et il y a des ombres effrayantes.

Look! There is a monster watching her with big yellow eyes. It has a huge mouth with sharp teeth.

But hold on, that's not a monster at all!

Regarde ! Il y a un monstre en train de la regarder avec de gros yeux jaunes. Il a une énorme bouche avec des dents pointues.

Mais attends, ce n'est pas du tout un monstre !

It is a woman from the village.

"Where are you going, little Susie?" the woman asks with a smile.

"I am going to the village to get some ingredients for a cake."

C'est une femme du village.

« Où vas-tu, petite Susie ? » demande la femme en souriant.

« Je vais au village acheter des ingrédients pour un gâteau.

And what is that behind the horses? She is scared of that big dragon watching her.

Et qu'est-ce c'est derrière les chevaux ? Elle a peur de ce gros dragon qui la regarde.

Susie continues on her way. She sees eyes watching her from the hayfield. That's scary!

Susie continue sa route. Mais elle voit des yeux la regarder depuis la prairie. C'est effrayant !

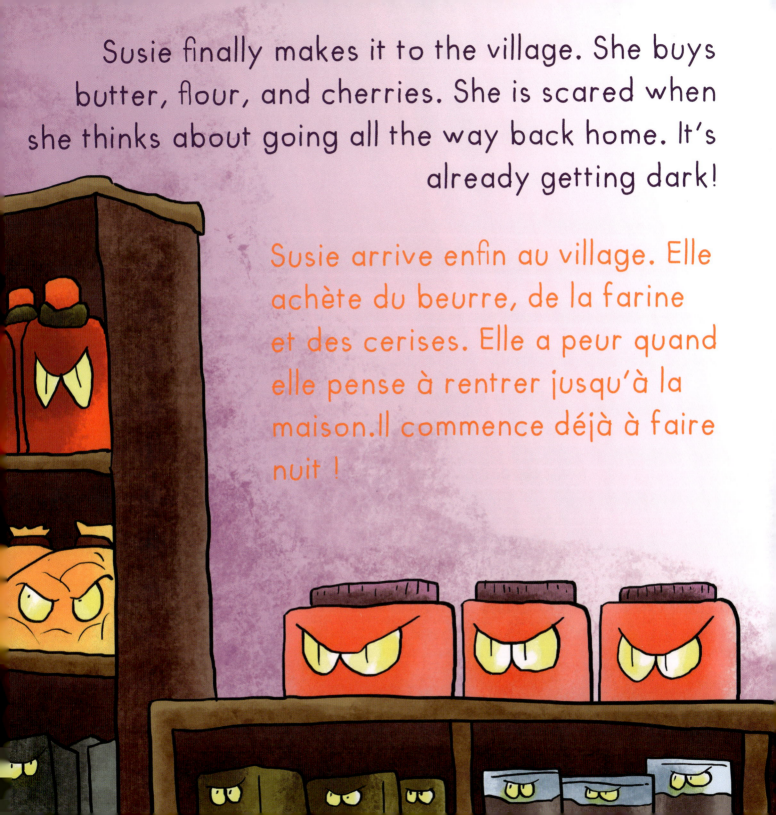

Susie finally makes it to the village. She buys butter, flour, and cherries. She is scared when she thinks about going all the way back home. It's already getting dark!

Susie arrive enfin au village. Elle achète du beurre, de la farine et des cerises. Elle a peur quand elle pense à rentrer jusqu'à la maison. Il commence déjà à faire nuit !

Susie is lucky! Her grandpa comes along the way with his bicycle. He lets her sit on the back. So they can go home together!

Elle a de la chance ! Son grand-père la rejoint sur le chemin avec son vélo. Il la laisse s'asseoir à l'arrière. Ainsi ils peuvent rentrer à la maison ensemble !

Ils passent les bottes de foin dans le champ, mais il n'y a pas d'yeux qui les regardent. Ils rencontrent aussi le loup, qui est juste un petit chien.

Ils s'arrêtent près des chevaux pour les nourrir.
Il n'y a pas de dragon dans les parages.

They see the friendly woman. They ride through the dark forest with the mysterious shadows and across the field with the scarecrows.

But where are the scarecrows?

Ils voient la gentille femme dans la forêt, ils traversent la forêt sombre avec les ombres effrayantes et le champ avec les épouvantail.

Mais où sont les épouvantails ?

Où sont tous les monstres que j'ai vus ?
Susie est étonnée.

She realizes they are all gone. "It is all imagination," her grandpa says. Susie understands and thinks

I can handle my fears!

Elle se rend compte qu'ils ont tous disparu. « C'est tout de l'imagination », dit son grand-père. Susie comprend. Elle pense :

je peux faire face à mes peurs !

COLORING PICS

Bilingual Books to Remember

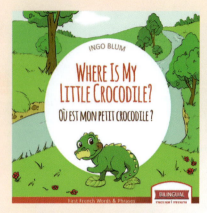
ISBN 979-8685008831

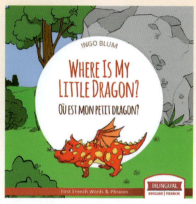
ISBN 979-8685346599

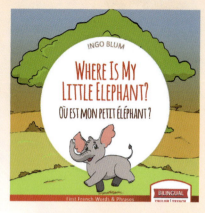
ISBN 979-8685353610

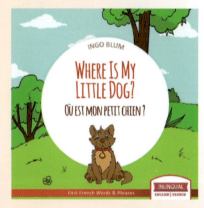
ISBN 979-8685016423

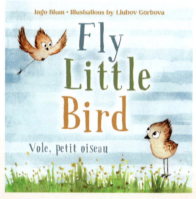
ISBN 979-8598437162

Follow me

 ingoblumauthor

 ingosplanet

 ingosplanet

Get my 5 eBook Starter Library in English for FREE on bit.ly/5freebooks